Hindu Festivals
Through the Year

Anita Ganeri

W
FRANKLIN WATTS
LONDON • SYDNEY

This edition 2007

First published in 2003 by Franklin Watts

Franklin Watts
338 Euston Road
London NW1 3BH

Franklin Watts Australia
Hachette Children's Books
Level 17/207 Kent Street
Sydney, NSW 2000

A CIP catalogue record for this book is available
from the British Library.

Dewey number 294.5

ISBN 978 0 7496 7364 2

Printed in China

Franklin Watts is a division of Hachette Children's Books.

Editor: Kate Banham   Designer: Joelle Wheelwright
Art Direction: Jonathan Hair   Illustrations: Peter Bull
Picture Research: Diana Morris   Educational Consultant: Alan Brown
Faith Consultant: Rasamandala Das (ISKCON)

Picture Credits:
Eric Bach/Britstock-IFA: front cover, 6, 26; B. Dhanjal/Trip: 19t; Dinodia/Trip: 12,
13t, 17, 20b, 21t; Chris Fairclough/Franklin Watts: 10, 23, 25b; F. Good/Trip: 8,
9t; H. Luther/Trip: 22b; Christine Osborne/World Religions Photo Library: 9b, 11,
27b; H. Rogers/Trip: 15t, 18, 25, 27c; Steve Shott/Franklin Watts: 7, 14, 19, 20t,
21b, 22t, 24; V&A Museum/Bridgeman Art Library: 16.

Contents

Words printed in **bold** are explained in the glossary.

Introduction

Hindus are people who follow the religion of Hinduism. They call their tradition *sanatana dharma*, which is **Sanskrit** for 'eternal teaching'. Today, there are about 800 million Hindus. Most live in India, where Hinduism began at least 4,500 years ago. But there are Hindu communities all over the world, especially in Britain and North America.

Hindus consider the River Ganges to be sacred. Many pilgrims come to bathe in its holy waters.

The Hindu calendar

The Hindu calendar is based on the moon. Each of the 12 months is divided into a 'bright half' (from the new moon to the full moon), and a 'dark half' (from the full moon to the next new moon). The months are 29 or 30 days long, giving a year of 354 days. The Western, or everyday, calendar is based on the sun and has 365 days. To bring the two calendars into line, an extra month is added every few years. (See page 28 for the names of the Hindu months.)

Hindu teachings

Hinduism has many ways of worship, but most Hindus share the same basic teachings. They believe in a great and eternal spirit, called **Brahman**, the invisible force behind all creation. Sometimes Hindus call Brahman God. Sometimes Hindus worship God in the form of deities (gods or goddesses), who represent different aspects of Brahman's power (see opposite). Hindus believe that every living thing has a soul, called *atman*. When you die, your soul is **reincarnated** in another body. This happens again and again until, by leading a good life, you break free and reach *moksha*, or freedom.

How Hindus worship

Hindus worship at home and in the **mandir** (temple). Worship is called *puja*. Hindus pray, chant verses from the sacred texts and make offerings of flowers, fruit and sweets to a **murti** (sacred image) which represents God or a particular deity. In return, they hope to receive the deity's blessing.

.........................➤

Music is an important part of worship. The drum, bells and tambourine are traditional Indian instruments.

Some of the main Hindu deities

Balarama	The elder brother of Lord Krishna. He grew up with Krishna in Vrindavan.	**Lakshmi**	The goddess of beauty, wealth and good fortune. Lakshmi is the wife of Lord Vishnu.
Brahma	One of the three main gods of Hinduism. The creator of the universe.	**Parvati**	The main form of the mother goddess. Parvati is the beautiful wife of Lord Shiva and mother of Ganesha.
Durga	The ten-armed goddess of war. In her arms, she carries weapons given to her by the gods. She rides on a lion or tiger.	**Radha**	A milkmaid from Vrindavan who became Lord Krishna's wife.
Ganesha	The elephant-headed god of wisdom and good fortune. Ganesha is the son of Lord Shiva and Parvati. Hindus pray to Ganesha before starting any task because he is believed to remove obstacles.	**Rama**	Lord Rama is the seventh avatar of Lord Vishnu. He is a prince and the hero of the *Ramayana.*
		Saraswati	The goddess of learning and the arts, and the wife of Lord Brahma.
Indra	The king of the gods and the god of rain which makes the crops grow. He is sometimes called Bhogi.	**Shiva**	One of the three main gods of Hinduism. The destroyer of evil in the universe.
		Sita	The wife of Lord Rama.
Kama	The god of love. He is sometimes described as a handsome man, riding on a parrot or cuckoo and carrying a bow and arrows.	**Skanda**	The son of Lord Shiva, and brother of Ganesha. He is often shown with six heads. He is leader of the gods' army.
		Subhadra	Lord Krishna's sister.
Krishna	One of the most popular Hindu gods. Lord Krishna is the eighth *avatar* of Lord Vishnu who grew up as a cowherd boy in Vrindavan. He is sometimes called Jagannath.	**Surya**	The sun god, the source of heat and life.
		Vishnu	One of the three main gods of Hinduism. The protector of the universe.
		Yama	The Hindu god of death.

Pongal

In mid-January, the great harvest festival of *Pongal* is celebrated in South India. In other parts of India, it is called *Makar Sankranti* and *Lohri*. The festival lasts for three days. *Pongal* is a happy time when people thank God for the rice and sugarcane harvest, and for the sun, the Earth and their cattle. A special *Pongal puja* is held, and friends and neighbours share a great feast to celebrate.

.......................➤

This Hindu girl has drawn a *kolam* pattern outside her house.

Honouring Indra

The first day of *Pongal* is called *Bhogi Pongal* and is dedicated to the god, Indra (Bhogi). He is the god of clouds and rain which make the crops grow. This is a family day when houses are spring-cleaned and decorated with colourful patterns, called *kolam*, drawn with rice-flour paste. People also light bonfires in front of their houses and burn any useless, or worn-out objects. This marks the clearing out of the old, and the welcoming in of the new.

Worshipping the sun

The second day of *Pongal* is *Surya Pongal*, a time for worshipping Surya, god of the sun. People perform *puja* to Surya in return for his blessings on their land and crops. They also make offerings of sweet rice pudding, called *pongal*, from which the festival gets its name.

Festival of cattle

The third day of *Pongal* is *Mattu Pongal*, the festival of cattle. To Hindus, cows are sacred animals because they give milk, a precious source of food. Hindus will not harm or kill a cow, nor eat beef. On *Mattu Pongal*, farmers honour their cattle by painting their horns and decorating them with bells and garlands. The cattle are fed with boiled rice and allowed to roam wherever they like.

Boiling over

Offerings of fruit and rice pudding (*pongal*).

The word 'pongal' is the name of the special sweet rice pudding eaten at the festival. It also means 'boiling over' because of the way in which the *pongal* is cooked. First sugarcane is crushed and boiled to make jaggery (sugar syrup). Milk is heated until it boils, then the rice and jaggery are added. As it cooks, the *pongal* is allowed to boil over and spill out of the pot, hence its name.

Cows are especially honoured at *Pongal*.

Vasanta Panchami

The festival of *Vasanta Panchami* is celebrated in north India in January or February. It marks the end of winter and the first day of spring. The name of the festival means 'the fifth day of spring' because it falls on the fifth day of the bright half of the month of *Magha*.

Saraswati Puja

In some parts of India, the festival is known as *Saraswati Puja*. People visit the mandir and perform *puja* to Saraswati, goddess of the arts, learning and wisdom. This is believed to be a good day for children to begin their education. Young children may be given a pen or piece of chalk and taught how to write the alphabet.

A paper garland

Hindus offer garlands to the deities, holy people and guests, as a sign of respect and welcome.

To make a garland for Saraswati Puja:

1. Make some flowers out of yellow paper.
2. Thread a needle with a length of thread about a metre long.
3. Push the needle through the centre of each flower.
4. Tie the ends of the thread together and your garland is ready.

Wearing yellow

Many Hindus wear bright yellow clothes on the day of *Saraswati Puja* because yellow is the colour of spring. They offer yellow flowers to God, and put yellow **tilaks** (marks of blessing) on their foreheads.

◄ ....
People wear garlands of yellow flowers for many festivals, including *Saraswati Puja*.

Mahashivaratri

In February or March, the festival of *Mahashivaratri* is held to honour Shiva, one of the main Hindu deities. The word 'shivaratri' means 'night of Shiva', and 'maha' means 'great'. Shiva is considered to be the destroyer of evil in the world. According to legend, his home is a high mountain in the **Himalayas**.

This statue shows *Shiva Nataraja* (dancing Shiva).

On Shiva's forehead is the third eye of knowledge.

The trident is a symbol of destruction.

The circle of flame represents the never-ending cycle of time.

Lord of the dance

Legend says, that on the night of *Mahashivaratri*, Shiva performs a special dance, called the cosmic dance of creation. In this dance, Shiva destroys the old world and creates a new one. His dance represents the energy flowing through the world which gives the seasons, day and night, and birth and death.

Praising Shiva

Followers of Shiva spend the whole night in the mandir, listening to stories about Shiva and singing Shiva's praises. Next day, a special ceremony takes place. Worshippers pour milk, water or honey over a small stone column, called a *lingam*, which represents Shiva. Many people also **fast** for 24 hours.

Holi

One of the happiest and most colourful festivals in the Hindu year is *Holi*. It falls in February or March, and marks the beginning of spring. Traditionally, *Holi* was when farmers celebrated the first wheat harvest of the year. There are many legends about *Holi*. One of the most famous tells the story of a prince, called Prahlad, and Holika, a wicked witch, after whom the festival is named (see below). Another tells of Lord Krishna. You can read this story on page 14.

At *Holi*, people offer lucky coconuts to the gods.

The story of *Holi*

There was once a wicked king, called Hiranyakashipu, who ordered people to stop worshipping God but to worship him instead. His son, Prahlad, refused to obey his orders. In a fury, the king tried to kill his son. He threw him into a pit of poisonous snakes, then ordered an elephant to charge at him. But nothing worked. Each time Lord Vishnu protected Prahlad.

Then the king's sister, a witch called Holika, had a plan. She tricked Prahlad into walking into a bonfire with her. Holika had magical powers which stopped her getting burned and she told Prahlad that she would protect him. Just in time, Lord Vishnu snatched Prahlad out of the flames and took away Holika's powers so that she perished instead.

Holi bonfires

On the first night of *Holi*, people build huge bonfires to remember the story of Holika. It also reminds them of Prahlad's faith in God and of the triumph of good over evil. At dusk, they gather round the fire, and the priest says prayers and lights the fire. Then people throw offerings of coconuts, popcorn and rice into the flames. They believe that the fire will carry the offerings up to God, in return for God's blessings. Sometimes, an **effigy** of Holika is burnt. Later, the roasted coconuts are split open and eaten.

Ashes from the *Holi* bonfire are said to protect people against disease.

Holi legend

Another legend linked with *Holi* tells how the goddess, Parvati, fell in love with Lord Shiva and wanted to marry him. But Shiva did not notice her. Kama, the god of love, decided to help her. But as he shot his arrow of love, Shiva opened his third eye of destruction and burned Kama to ashes. Later, Parvati brought Kama back to life, on the day celebrated as *Holi*.

Kama, the Hindu god of love, is often shown riding on a parrot.

Celebrating Holi

This very popular festival is celebrated all over India and in other countries where Hindus have settled. In India, the festival usually lasts for at least two or three days, and sometimes for a week. In Britain, it lasts for one day only. The weather is usually colder but people gather around bonfires lit in local parks. Wherever it is celebrated, *Holi* is a time for having fun.

Krishna with his companion, Radha. Krishna's practical jokes are often remembered at *Holi*.

The story of Krishna

Another story associated with *Holi* is about Lord Krishna's childhood. Krishna is one of the most popular Hindu deities, famous for his mischief-making and for playing tricks on his friends. Krishna was brought up by a cowherd and his wife. His constant companions were the beautiful Radha, and her friends, the *gopis* (milkmaids). For fun, Krishna drenched Radha with coloured water and stole the *gopis*' clothes as they bathed. At *Holi*, Hindus remember Krishna's antics and offer *puja* to Krishna and Radha.

Coloured powders

Today, at *Holi*, people still soak each other in coloured powders, mixed with water. They buy the powders from stalls set up in the streets. They use a range of objects, from plastic bottles to water pistols and bicycle pumps, to spray the colours on. By the end of the day, everyone is drenched. Later on, people get out of their wet clothes, scrub off the colours, and change into their best clothes. They spend the evening visiting friends and family with gifts of delicious sweets.

At *Holi*, everyone gets covered in coloured powder and paste.

Holi sweets

Hindus eat many types of Indian sweets at *Holi*. Some people buy sweets from sweet shops; others make them at home. One of the most popular is coconut *barfi*.

A selection of Indian sweets.

To make coconut barfi:
You will need
1/2 litre milk
1 kg granulated sugar
2 tablespoons butter
1 kg dried milk powder
1 cup dessicated coconut
1/2 cup chopped nuts

1. Heat the milk and sugar in a saucepan until it boils.

2. Add the butter. Stir until it melts.

3. Add the coconut and nuts. Turn off the heat.

4. Stir in the milk powder.

5. Spread the mixture on to a lightly greased baking tray.

6. Leave it to cool, then cut it into squares.

Ramanavami

In March or April, Hindus celebrate the birthday of Lord Rama. This festival is called *Ramanavami*, which means 'Rama ninth', because it falls on the ninth day of the bright half of *Chaitra*. On this day, Rama is said to have been born in the town of Ayodhya in northern India.

Rama's birthday

At *Ramanavami*, many Hindus go to the mandir to listen to readings from the *Ramayana*, the long poem which tells the story of Rama's life (see page 24). An image of the baby Rama is placed in a cradle and covered up. At midday, when Rama is said to have been born, the covering is taken off. People sing songs and rock the cradle. In Ayodhya, Rama's birthplace, images of Rama and his wife, Sita, are taken out of the mandir and carried through the streets.

Saving the world

Hindus believe that Rama and Krishna are avatars of Lord Vishnu. 'Avatar' means 'incarnation in visible form'. Lord Vishnu has come down to Earth in nine different forms to save the world from evil. His tenth avatar is yet to come. The ten avatars are:

1. Matsya, the fish
2. Kurma, the tortoise
3. Varaha, the boar
4. Narasimha, the man-lion
5. Vamana, the dwarf
6. Parashurama, the warrior
7. Lord Rama, the ideal king
8. Lord Krishna, the cowherd boy
9. Lord Buddha, the teacher
10. Kalki, a rider on a white horse, who is yet to come

This painting shows Vishnu in the centre of his ten avatars.

Ratha Yatra

Every year, in June or July, a great procession takes place in the city of Puri in north-eastern India. It is called *Ratha Yatra*, which means 'the journey of the chariot'. A huge chariot is pulled through the streets, carrying three sacred images. The main one is Jagannath, the Lord of the Universe. Jagannath is another name for Lord Krishna. The other two are Krishna's sister, Subhadra, and his brother, Balarama.

A Prayer to Lord Jagannath

'When Lord Jagannath is on his *Ratha Yatra* chariot ... people loudly chant prayers and songs. Hearing their songs, Lord Jagannath feels kindly towards them. He is the ocean of mercy and the true friend of all the world ... O Lord Jagannath, Lord of the Universe, kindly become visible to my eyes.'

Festival chariot

The chariots used to pull the sacred images are huge wooden carts, many metres high and with up to 16 wheels. Hundreds, or even thousands, of worshippers take turns to pull the carts, and this is considered a great honour. (In English, large lorries are called juggernauts because they are similar in size to Lord Jagannath's chariot.) *Ratha Yatra* is also celebrated in many towns and cities outside India. Each summer, there is a *Ratha Yatra* procession through central London, England.

← A *Ratha Yatra* procession in Puri, India.

Raksha Bandhan

The festival of *Raksha Bandhan* takes place in August. This is a special time for Hindu brothers and sisters when they show their love for each other and promise to look after each other. *Raksha Bandhan* is celebrated all over India and in other countries where Hindus have settled. If people do not have brothers or sisters, it does not matter. In Hindu families, cousins and very close family friends count as brothers and sisters, too.

This Hindu girl is tying a *rakhi* around her brother's wrist.

Brothers and sisters

On *Raksha Bandhan*, girls perform a special ceremony. First the girl says a prayer to ask God to look after her brother. Then she makes a mark with red powder on his forehead. This is a *tilak*, a sign of blessing. Next she ties a colourful bracelet, called a *rakhi*, around her brother's right wrist to protect him from evil. This is where the festival gets its name. 'Raksha' means 'protection' and 'Bandhan' means 'to tie'. In return, the brother promises to look after his sister in the coming year. At the end of the ceremony, the brother gives his sister a gift of money or jewellery. Brothers are supposed to wear their *rakhis* until the thread breaks.

Raksha Bandhan stories

There are many stories explaining how *Raksha Bandhan* began. One story tells of a war between the gods and the demons. A demon king, called Bali, fought Indra, king of the gods, and drove him out of his kingdom. Indra's wife asked Lord Vishnu for help. He gave her a silk bracelet to tie around Indra's wrist to keep Indra safe. When Bali and Indra fought again, the bracelet protected Indra. He defeated the demon and won his kingdom back.

Another story tells of a great warrior, Abhimanyu, whose grandmother gave him a *rakhi* to wear. While he was wearing it, he could not be harmed. But when the *rakhi* broke in battle, Abhimanyu was killed.

Many Hindu women buy ready-made *rakhis* from market stalls. They send them by post to brothers who live far away.

Making a *rakhi*

There are hundreds of different types of *rakhi*, made from twisted thread or ribbon, and decorated with beads, tinsel, sequins and pompoms.

To make a rakhi:

1. Cut a piece of brightly coloured ribbon, long enough to go around your wrist.
2. Cut a small circle out of card and stick it on to the ribbon, halfway along its length.
3. Decorate the card with shiny sequins, tiny beads, glitter or tinsel.

A shop-bought *rakhi*.

Janmashtami

In August or September, Hindus celebrate Lord Krishna's birthday with a festival called *Janmashtami*. This means 'eighth day of birth' because it falls on the eighth night of the dark half of the month of *Badra*. Like Rama, Krishna is an avatar of Vishnu. Legend says that, when Krishna was born, his wicked uncle, King Kamsa, wanted to kill him. But Krishna's father rescued his son and took him across the river to safety in the village of Vrindavan. There he was brought up by a cowherd and his wife.

Statue of Krishna the cowherd.

Birthday celebrations

At *Janmashtami*, ceremonies acting out Krishna's birth are held in mandirs devoted to Krishna. It is said that Krishna was born at midnight and so people stay up late to welcome him. They sing songs, called **bhajans**, in praise of Krishna, dance and make offerings. An image of the baby Krishna is placed in a cradle, covered with a silk cloth. At midnight, the cover is taken off and worshippers take turns to rock the cradle. There is also an **arti** ceremony, in which a tray of lamps is circled in front of the deity to welcome him.

In Mumbai, India, people celebrate *Janmashtami* by making a human pyramid.

Ganesha Chaturthi

The festival of *Ganesha Chaturthi* celebrates the birthday of the elephant-headed god, Ganesha. 'Chaturthi' means 'fourth day' because it falls on the fourth day of the bright half of the month of *Badra* (August/September).

Ganesha

Ganesha is a very special god for Hindus. They believe that he removes obstacles and always worship him before performing any *puja*, starting any new task or going on a journey. *Ganesha Chaturthi* is especially popular in western India. In Mumbai, India, people worship huge clay images of Ganesha and make offerings of flowers and sweets. Then the images are paraded around the city, accompanied by music and dancing, and immersed in the sea.

↑ *Ganesha Chaturthi* parade in Mumbai.

Prayer to Ganesha

'O Lord Ganesha, with a curved trunk and large body, Glowing with the brilliance of a million suns, Make my work free of obstacles, always.'

Cursing the moon

In some places, people believe that it is unlucky to look at the moon on *Ganesha Chaturthi*. Ganesha was famous for his big appetite. A story tells how once he was invited to a great feast with the gods. He ate so many *laddus* (sweets) that he toppled over when he tried to stand up. Seeing this, the moon began laughing. Ganesha was furious, and cursed the moon, and everyone who looked at it on this day.

Festivals of the Goddess

Some Hindus choose to worship God in the form of a mother goddess. She has many different names to show the different sides of her character. Her main form is as Parvati, the wife of Lord Shiva. In her fierce form, she is known as Durga, the goddess of war. In September or October, three festivals are held to honour her. They are called *Navaratri*, *Durga Puja* and *Dassehra*.

▲ Statue of Durga, the fierce form of the goddess.

These women are performing the stick dance (*dandia ras*) for *Navaratri*. ▲

Nine nights

The name 'Navaratri' means 'nine nights' because the festival lasts for the first nine nights of the bright half of *Ashvina*. Over the nine nights, the mother goddess is sometimes worshipped in nine different forms. *Puja* is performed and some people fast, eating only fruit and milk. A special feature of the festival is the *dandia ras*, or 'stick dance'. Dancers each have two sticks and dance around each other, faster and faster, banging their sticks against those of the other dancers.

Durga Puja

The festival of *Durga Puja* falls towards the end of *Navaratri*. This is when Hindus remember the story of how Durga fought and killed the evil demon, Mahisha, who was disguised as a huge buffalo. The gods had told him that he could not be killed, except by a woman. At *Durga Puja*, people celebrate this triumph of good over evil.

The tenth day

The day after *Navaratri* is called *Dassehra*, or 'tenth day'. Apart from worshipping Durga, this is also a time when some Hindus remember Rama's victory over the evil demon king, Ravana. You can read this story on page 24. During *Dassehra*, groups of actors tour towns and villages, performing a play of the story, called the *Rama Lila*. The festival ends in dramatic style. A huge model of Ravana is made out of straw and papier-mâché. This is filled with fireworks, then set alight with an enormous bang.

Rama Lila being acted out.

Shadow show

In some places, shadow puppets are used to act out the *Rama Lila*. Read the story of Rama on page 24, then try staging your own shadow show.

To make a shadow theatre:

1. Make a screen from a cardboard box. Cut out the front and back, and stick a piece of white cloth across the back. Put your screen on a table.
2. Draw the outline of the puppets onto dark card and cut them out. Make sure they fit your screen.
3. Tape a thin stick to the back of each puppet.
4. Place a reading lamp on a chair behind the screen, so that it shines on the white sheet.
5. Sit between the lamp and the screen and use the sticks to move your puppets behind the white sheet. Your audience will see their shadows on the other side.

Divali

In October or November, Hindus everywhere celebrate the festival of *Divali*. There are many different reasons why *Divali* is celebrated. According to one of the ancient Hindu calendars, it is the start of the New Year. At *Divali*, people also worship Lakshmi, the goddess of good fortune and wealth. During this time many Hindus also remember the story of Rama and his wife, Sita. This is told in the *Ramayana*, one of the most sacred of all the Hindu texts.

Statues of Rama (centre) and Sita (right), with Lakshman (left) and Hanuman (front left).

The story of Rama

Long ago, Prince Rama was born in Ayodhya. Rama was heir to his father's throne but his step-mother wanted her son to be king instead. So Rama was sent to live in the forest for 14 years, with his wife, Sita, and brother, Lakshman. One day, Sita was kidnapped by Ravana, the evil, 10-headed demon king. He carried her off to his palace on the island of Lanka. In despair, Rama called upon his friend, Hanuman, the monkey general. With a huge army of monkeys and bears, they set off for Lanka to rescue Sita. A terrible battle raged. Finally, Rama met Ravana, and killed him with a golden arrow, a gift from the gods. In triumph, Rama and Sita returned to Ayodhya, to claim their rightful throne.

Goddess of wealth

Divali is also a time for worshipping the goddess, Lakshmi. She is Lord Vishnu's wife, and the goddess of good fortune and wealth. At *Divali*, Hindus welcome Lakshmi into their homes, in the hope that she will bring happiness and prosperity. Images of Lakshmi show her with four arms, each representing one of her qualities or powers. In two of her hands she holds lotus flowers, signs of purity. The upraised palm of her third hand protects her followers. Gold coins, a sign of riches, fall from her fourth hand.

Lakshmi is often shown standing in a lotus flower.

Festival of lights

The name 'Divali' comes from the word 'Deepavali' which means 'rows of lights'. At *Divali*, Hindus decorate their homes and mandirs with small clay lamps, filled with oil. These are called *divas*. Sometimes strings of fairy lights are used instead of *divas*. The lamps are intended to welcome Lakshmi into people's houses, and to guide Rama and Sita safely home on the night of the new moon.

In the mandir, everyone offers lamps in front of the gods' shrine.

Celebrating Divali

This is one of the most popular festivals in the Hindu year. In India, it lasts for five days, each with its own customs and ceremonies. Schools and offices are closed, and people enjoy a holiday. In other countries, such as Britain, *Divali* is celebrated in the mandir on the nearest weekend. To mark this happy occasion, people exchange gifts of jewellery and new clothes, *Divali* cards and boxes of delicious sweets. Apart from the story of Rama and Sita, each of the *Divali* days also has its own story.

Divali begins

On the first day of *Divali*, many Hindus light a single *diva* and place it with the flame pointing south, as an offering to Yama, the Hindu god of death.

On the second day, they get up early, bathe and put on clean clothes. This is the day for remembering another *Divali* story, when Krishna defeated the demon, Narakasur.

In the evening, spectacular displays of fireworks light up the night sky. The fireworks are set off to ward off evil.

◄··············

Lighting *diva* lamps reminds people how light drives away darkness and God destroys evil.

Lakshmi Puja

The third day of *Divali* is a time for worshipping Lakshmi. In the evening, families get together for a special *puja*. For business people, this day marks the end of the old financial year. Accounts are settled, and old accounts books are closed and offered to Lakshmi. New accounts books, sometimes decorated with pictures of Lakshmi, are opened the next day.

New beginnings

The fourth day of *Divali* is a day for new beginnings. Many people celebrate by wearing new clothes. They also remember the story of how Lord Vishnu appeared on Earth in the form of a dwarf to defeat a wicked king, called Bali.

The last day of *Divali* is 'Sisters' Day', when brothers visit their sisters' homes for a delicious meal. It is said that the god, Yama, visited his sister on this day, and ordered everyone to do the same.

Closing the old year's accounts books at *Lakshmi Puja*.

Rangoli patterns

Another way of welcoming Lakshmi into people's homes is to draw a beautiful *rangoli* pattern on the doorstep. These patterns are drawn using coloured chalk, sand, rice or flour. In the centre, there is often a lotus flower, a symbol of Lakshmi.

In the West, some mandirs hold *rangoli* competitions for children. The best design wins a prize.

In the centre of this colourful *rangoli* pattern is the symbol for the sacred sound 'om'. Many people chant this to help them think deeply about their faith.

Festival Calendar

Month	Event
Magha	Pongal
Magha	Vasanta Panchami/ Saraswati Puja
Phalguna	Mahashivaratri
Phalguna	Holi
Chaitra	Ramanavami
Ashadha	Ratha Yatra
Shravana	Raksha Bandhan
Badra	Janmashtami
Badra	Ganesha Chaturthi
Ashvina	Navaratri
Ashvina	Durga Puja
Ashvina	Dassehra
Karttika	Divali

Hindu months

The months of the Hindu year are:

Magha	(January/February)
Phalguna	(February/March)
Chaitra	(March/April)
Vaishakha	(April/May)
Jyeshtha	(May/June)
Ashadha	(June/July)
Shravana	(July/August)
Badra	(August/September)
Ashvina	(September/October)
Karttika	(October/November)
Margashirsha	(November/December)
Pausha	(December/January)

Glossary

Arti A ceremony in which a tray of lamps is offered to a deity, as a sign of welcome.

Atman The individual soul inside each living thing.

Avatar One who descends. The descent of a deity to Earth. Lord Vishnu has descended to Earth nine times. His avatars include Lord Rama and Lord Krishna.

Bhajans Religious hymns or songs sung in praise of God.

Brahman The great spirit. Brahman is invisible, eternal and everywhere. Everything comes from Brahman and eventually returns to Brahman. Hindus sometimes call Brahman God.

Effigy A model or statue.

Fast To go without food.

Himalayas A range of very high mountains across the north of India.

Mandir A place where Hindus go to worship. It is also called a temple.

Moksha The freedom of the soul (*atman*) from the cycle of reincarnation. The aim of a Hindu's life.

Murti A sacred image of a deity. It stands in the inner chamber of the mandir and represents God.

Puja The main Hindu form of worship. Prayers, flowers, food and incense are offered to the deities.

Ramayana The long poem which tells the story of Rama and Sita. It is one of the most sacred Hindu texts.

Reincarnation The cycle of birth, death and rebirth. Hindus believe that, when you die, your soul is reborn in another body.

Sanatana dharma Eternal law or teaching. The name Hindus give to their teachings or beliefs.

Sanskrit An ancient Indian language and the sacred language of Hinduism.

Tilak A mark made on a person's forehead as a sign of blessing or welcome.

Further Resources

Books

A World of Festivals: Holi and Divali
Dilip Kadodwala, Evans Brothers, 1997

Storyteller: Hindu Stories
Anita Ganeri, Evans Brothers, 2001

What do we know about Hinduism?
Anita Ganeri, Hodder Wayland, 1995

Celebration!
Barnabas and Annabel Kindersley, Dorling Kindersley, 1997

Festivals in World Religions
The Shap Working Party on World Religions in Education, 1998

World Religions: Hinduism
Katherine Prior, Franklin Watts 1999

Beliefs and Cultures: Hindu
Anita Ganeri, Franklin Watts 1996

Websites

www.festivals.com
Festivals, holy days and holidays.

www.indiancultureonline.com
All aspects of Hinduism and Hindu festivals.

www.hindunet.org
More facts about festivals and about Hinduism.

www.hindunewyear.com
Information about Hindu new year celebrations.

In Australia you can check out the Hindu Council of Australia at **www.hinducouncil.com.au**, and the Hindu Foundation of Australia at **www.hindunet. com.au/hindu_foundation.htm**.

Index